CW01391334

THE WONDER OF SWIMMING

Happy 1st Birthday
Summer
Have fun swimming!
Love & hugs,
Jess x

Author: Debra Franks
Design and illustration: Adrian Franks & Alexander Franks

First published 2022

Publisher: Debra Franks
65 Queen Alexandra Road, Salisbury, Wiltshire SP2 9LL
www.wonderofswimming.co.uk

© Debra Franks 2022
All rights reserved. No part of this publication may be reproduced, stored
in a retrieval system or transmitted in any form or by any means, electronic,
mechanical, photocopying, recording or otherwise, without prior
permission from the author and publisher.

Printed in England

ISBN No: 978 1 3999 2111 4

THE WONDER OF SWIMMING

Debra Franks

The Wonder of Swimming is only possible because of the children I have taught over the years. The magic and wonder found in these pages is all down to those children and their incredible imaginations.

Together we had a lot of fun and I hope this book helps children, parents and carers to see why we teach the things we do.

Hi, I'm Poppy and today I'm having my first swimming lesson.

It's my first time and all a bit new for me.

I wonder what it will be like?

How deep will the water be?

What will my teacher be like?

What will my classmates be like?

Where do mummy and daddy go while I'm swimming?

What will I have to do in the lesson?

That's a lot of questions... lets have some fun and find out.

The pool environment

This is what our pool looks like.

Big pool

Small pool

Beach pool

Register

First, I meet my teacher who is called Debbie.
Then I meet my classmates, Charlie and Jasmine.

The teacher takes the register.

We all wear red swimming hats.
This is so the Lifeguards know we
are new swimmers.

What are Lifeguards?
Lifeguards are people you see around
the pool who look out for all the
swimmers and help to keep us safe.

We are starting in the small pool
where I can stand up in the water.

Pool entry

We can enter the pool by the steps.

Or we can walk backwards down the ladder.

Or at the side of the pool, where we make a triangle with our hands, turn onto our tummies and slide in slowly.

Leg kick / ballerina and football feet

We sit on the side of the pool or on the steps
and practice our ballerina feet and football feet.

Poolside movement / monkeying along

When we go down the steps we become monkeys on the side of the pool.

It's fun hanging on as we monkey along.

Breathing out / bubbles

We hold hands and sing 'Ring o' Roses' and we all fall down.

Some of us blow bubbles like a whale.

We blow a butterfly from our hands.

Or we snort like a noisy pig while underwater.

Water confidence / rain showers

We might pretend to take a shower.

Or we wash the breakfast away from our faces.

Moving around the pool / animals

We can move around the pool being all sorts of animals.

I like being a jumping kangaroo, a bunny or a crab.

Arm movement / aeroplanes and submarines

Our arms can be aeroplanes and submarines.

They go high into the sky and down into
the water.

Body position and bubbles / crocodiles

Sometimes we are crocodiles on the steps.

We stretch out and roar noisily as we blow bubbles.

Push and glide body position and leg kick / rockets

Once we reach the side, we lie on our tummies and become rockets.

We blow bubbles, push off the wall and stretch into our rockets.

By kicking our legs, doing ballerina and football feet, we give our rockets an engine to go faster.

Submerging and diving / treasure

We go hunting for treasure like pirates.

Some of it floats on top of the water,
some treasure sinks under the water.

We need to become whales and blow bubbles
as we go underwater for the treasure.

Back work / wobbly jelly

At the steps we lie down.

It is a bit wobbly, like lying on a fruity jelly but it is soft like a pillow.

The water tickles my ears.

Recovery from back work to standing / sitting in a chair

We also practice sitting up in a chair.

We have to look at our feet,
bend our knees and sit up.

Then we get to lie back down.

Up and down.

Floating on our back / pink elephants

We relax on our backs and look up at the ceiling and see all sorts of wonders.

We see cobwebs and spiders, pink elephants and ladybirds.

Jasmine saw a light bulb!

We take turns to be a star in the water. 'Twinkle, twinkle little star'.

Turning over / pancakes

The teacher holds our heads while we float
and gently move our shoulders depending
which way we want to flip over.

'I'm a little pancake nice and flat,
flip me over just like that!'

When we flip ourselves over we blow bubbles.

End of lesson / splashy clap

At the end of the lesson we all give ourselves a special well done splashy clap.

Off to the showers / train driver

After our splashy clap we get to become a train and take turns to be the engine and drive our carriages to the showers.

This is where my mummy meets me after my swimming lesson.

Aim of the lesson / rockets

Our lesson had a lot of games and lots of magical fun.

We are all going to be really good rockets on our tummies and backs.

'Climb high climb far, your goal the sky, your aim the stars'

The author

Debra Franks was a swimming teacher for 12 years.

She trained and taught at Warminster pool, Salisbury swimming pool and Judy Sporle School of Swimming in Winchester, both privately and for County.

Debra is married with two boys, who both completed all levels of the Wiltshire swimming and life saving programmes.

Why we teach the things we do

We teach a combination of survival, water confidence and swimming. As teachers we want the children to breathe out when underwater, rather than breathe in, which is why we teach bubbles. We also want them to be able to hold onto the side and get to the steps – hence monkeying along the wall. To be able to twist their bodies, we teach pancakes to twist over onto their backs and to float.

When a child falls in the water we want them not to be shocked, to know what it feels like to have water on their faces and in their eyes which is why we teach without goggles to begin with.

What about goggles? I am all for them – have you ever tried to swim without them? When they are able to swim, or when they are seeking treasure, they will need goggles to see where they are going.

What about swimming aids? They are for safety and as an aid. But first we all need to learn about our own body balance, to be able to feel the instability the water can create and how to adjust our body to compensate. When you are one-to-one with your child in the swimming pool you are their safety aid, so give them the opportunity to discover their own body balance.

Have
fun
learning
to swim!

© 2022 Debra Franks

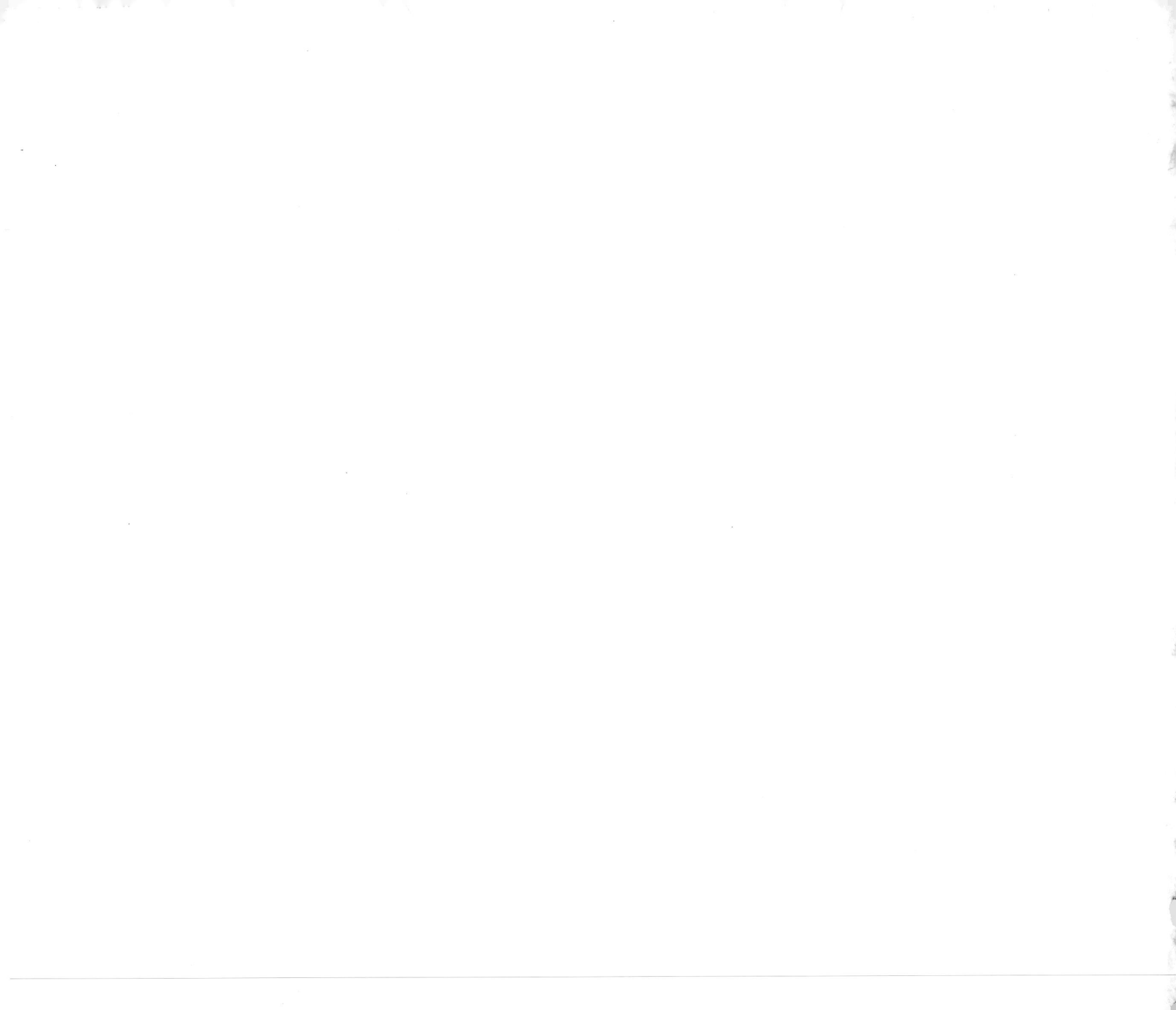